Bonfire

Bonfire

POEMS

Connie Wanek

Minnesota Voices Project Number 83

New Rivers Press 1997

© 1997 by Connie Wanek. All rights reserved
Library of Congress Catalog Number 97-65065
ISBN 0-89823-178-7
Edited by C. W. Truesdale
Copyedited by Joanne Fish
Cover painting, "The Minnesota St. Gang," by Patricia Canelake, oil on linen, 14 x 18 inches.
Cover design by Barb Patrie Graphic Design
Page design and typesetting by Interface Graphics, Inc.

New Rivers Press is a nonprofit literary press dedicated to publishing the very best emerging writers in our region, nation, and world.

The publication of *Bonfire* has been made possible by generous grants from the Jerome Foundation; the North Dakota Council on the Arts; the South Dakota Arts Council; Target Stores, Dayton's, and Mervyn's by the Dayton Hudson Foundation; and the James R. Thorpe Foundation.

Additional support has been provided by the Elmer L. and Eleanor J. Andersen Foundation, the Beim Foundation, the General Mills Foundation, Liberty State Bank, the McKnight Foundation, the Star Tribune/Cowles Media Company, the Tennant Company Foundation, and the contributing members of New Rivers Press. New Rivers is a member agency of United Arts.

Bonfire has been manufactured in the United States of America for New Rivers Press, 420 North 5th Street, Suite 910, Minneapolis, MN 55401. First Edition.

Printed on acid-free, recycled paper.

Visit our website: www.mtn.org/~newrivpr

For my family

Contents

Acknowledgments

Grateful acknowledgment is made to the following publications in which some of these poems first appeared: *The Virginia Quarterly Review*, *Poetry*, *Negative Capability*, *Country Journal*, *Poetry East*, *Cafe Solo*, *Green Mountains Review*, *Puerto del Sol*, *Plainsong*, *North Coast Review*, *Prairie Schooner*, *Ascent*, *The Seattle Review*, *Ruby*, *Loonfeather*, *Artword Quarterly*, and *The Wolf Head Quarterly*.

Additionally, the poem "Dragonfly" appeared in *Thirteen Broadsides*, an art exhibition (Spring 1996) sponsored by The Tweed Museum of Art in Duluth, Minnesota, as the collaborative text to a print by Adu Gindy.

Part One

April

When the snowbank dissolved
I found a comb and a muddy quarter.
I found the corpse of that missing mitten
still clutching some snow.

Then came snow with lightning,
beauty with a temper.
And sleet, the compromise that pleases no one;
precipitation by committee.

Out on Lake Superior the worried ice
paces up and down the shoreline
wearing itself out.

Chimneys have given up smoking.
In the balcony of the woods,
a soprano with feathers.

And upon the creek
the wicked spell is broken.
You are free to be water now.
You are free to go.

Red Fox

He lived all summer on the great man's estate,
the red fox, like a concubine.
The sight of him taking the bait
made the old gentleman tremble—
his modest toilette at the fountain
observed through binoculars,
his unmolested naps near the gray rock
where sunlight streamed through a dying birch.

Over and over the fox saw the old man hobble out
and fill the meat bowl. His was a pungent,
almost medical smell, that clung
like a tendril to the complicated air of human places.
At first each nerve objected. The fox
saw two dogs at the bay window, watching,
their coarse, domesticated faces
full of eager malevolence, like ex-wives.

Then overnight the sumac turned red.
The creeper suddenly blushed at its own rapaciousness.
How hard the wind tried to pick the trees up
but leaves only came away.
That summer, like all the others,
fled while the old man still wanted it, and the fox, too,
vanished into the copper-colored undergrowth
as into the magician's sleeve.

Wedding Pearls

1.

Mother's sentimental gift
hoarded these many years in her strongbox
like unfounded rumors of a brilliant ancestor.
Japanese pearls, the oyster's cloisonné,
an irritation that became in maturity
a pleasure, like a child.
They warm the hands that hold them.

These particular pearls—
acquired after the war when Mother, among others,
"rebuilt Japan." Photos reveal
confident, smiling giants,
missionaries of the Scandinavian work ethic:
"We have a better way to do that."
And among the ravaged inhabitants
those who must trade gems for rice.
Thus these pearls,
part of a dismembered estate,
humbly sold, so the legend goes;
these fifty-five identical orientals
knotted with silk. Bought to be
a counterweight to disaster.
Never worn, but slipped
from the brocade pouch
late at night, privately,
each creamy bead fingered
like an earlobe
or a baby's toe, so small, so perfect.

2.

The afternoon we walked to the jewelers'
was brilliant but cold.
Pearls in the pocket, concealed treasure,
and we strode down the crowded sidewalks
self-absorbed, like incognito
darlings of the paparazzi.
The pearls were yellow now,
little moons barely risen,
fifty-five full moons on a string . . .
more than four years, a baby born,
the elder four years closer to
possession of these pearls.
We spread them on the velvet before the appraiser.

He could tell with the merest glance
they were synthetic, glass to be exact.
He was rather synthetic himself,
those curls, that smile,
therefore we believed him immediately.
It's always the truth when we feel humbled.
For days we smiled ruefully at the foolishness
we inherited with the pearls,
the retribution of that long ago widow,
the new secret to keep from Mother,
the solace that we are only who we are
with no more than we have.

Abstract

The story begins a hundred years ago,
notations in that fine antique hand,
the getting and losing of a piece of land
ending with us.

Two wives became widows in this house,
walked from window to window looking out,
shrinking in their dresses,
padding their shoes with kleenex.
The lake was always there, the fog climbed the hill,
and the moon grew stout and thin
per the promissory note.

Teeth fell out, there was a divorce
(Solvieg got the house),
and at last the two children who fought so bitterly
had to "divide by equal shares, share and share alike"
the southerly 100 feet of lot 9 Endion Subdivision
together with all improvements.

It was the sister who stayed on.
It was she who saw the peonies through the dry year,
who took the broom to the wasp nest in the soffit,
who embraced those endless domestic economies,
and who penciled into the margins
padlock combinations, paint colors,
the Latin names of her perennials.

Her bones grew hollow like a bird's
so that when it was time to fly
she had only to spread her old wool shawl
and drop the ballast of this abstract.

Wild Apples

The tree is old, hidden behind
a veil of Virginia creeper,
the apples astringent, misshapen,
green with red tiger stripes,
misguided adornment or miracle
in the logged over third or fourth or fifth growth
along the creek. I gather a few windfalls,
too hard to bruise,
as I pass from nowhere to nowhere.

If I had roots I would put them down here.
Living roots, roots with feeling.
The apples are placed on the windowsill
where they can see out—
morning windows, sun coming out of the woods,
    disentangled.
How freely it floats before the clouds,
then willingly enters them.
And my daughter, scowling all day,
how she smiles when her friends come for her.

The hard brown boys find the apple tree
on one of their patrols
and load up on ammo.
One apple penetrates the storm window
but not the sash, and so glass separates
the curiously reunited offspring of the tree—
the litter brought together as dogs—
while the boys have of course scattered,
careening downhill on their bent bicycles.

The unburdened tree stands straighter,
smoothing the wrinkled skirt.
After all these years, some time apparently remains,
another evening, another autumn,
a tender half inch of growth on each arthritic branch.
Apples lay soft and brown in the underbrush,
waste and redundancy, windowsill apples
sitting on their weeping mold.

Once you took my picture under this very tree.
I was holding the child, who was holding wild apples.
Fourteen months, I wrote on the back.
She and I both looked pale after that first intense year,
milky, like the edge of the sky,
slightly translucent, slightly grave.
She was mine. She didn't belong to herself then.
It was September, just as it is now,
the sun listing to the south,
the hill's shadow crossing me at the knee.

The Girl and the Horses

I woke to find the gate open and the horses gone
and I thought, "What haven't I given you?"
Dawn was drying the gravel on the road;
the bridle I carried clinked against my knee.
They hadn't gone far. They stood at the corner
where the road turned toward infinite places
and raised their heads from their grazing to watch me.
I walked toward them, falsely confident,
like a teacher, unable to disguise
the nature of my duty.

The big roan played a vital part in my success,
turning his ears forward as he smelled sugar,
two white, pure, perfect cubes. And then,
because he had so often done so, he accepted the bit.
I drew him out of the ditch, two legs leading four,
seventy pounds leading seven hundred,
and the other horses, sighing and snorting, followed.
It looked as if we'd been on some field trip,
saw how money was made, or how trees
are stripped and turned into toilet paper.

That morning I thought myself lucky
and the beasts immeasurably foolish
as I led them back. All in, the gate locked,
I pulled the roan's head down to me
and slipped the bridle off, and he nipped me,
nipped me with his huge teeth, yellow as corn,
near my ear, and bolted into the pasture.

Bucket in the Well

Late afternoon, summer on the prairie,
the porch in shadow and the barn in full, strong light.
A thousand grasshoppers leap
as we walk through the tall grass near the river,
and we, like this water, slow and shallow
this time of year.

How I long to lie down in the grass
and sleep through many generations of grasshoppers!
Or climb into the loft—
here is where the cat has her young,
where the tom comes to kill them. Here is where
pigeon eggs roll from nests on the high beams.
Here is where a curious child played secretly with matches.

Here is where I lay me down,
rising only when the first snow blows through the
    knotholes.
The friendly straw, the horses rustling below,
the everlasting sleep that waits
to be filled, like the bucket at the bottom of the well.

A Child's Garden

These diapers on the clothesline, these signal flags,
concede the household's surrender to its child,
a toddler who gardens naked
debating whether to plant the seed or eat it.

She tips the packet upside down, sowing peas
in a heap, as one pours sugar into tea,
with the wind, oh lovely wind, stirring.

Slim without her diaper,
she's white as a root above the brown earth,
a small person with a will so strong,
with impulses of the most desperate sort.

A gust blows apple petals over her shoulders—
the tree exquisitely attired
in a pink-white wedding dress with pearls.

And now the bride studies her little niece
as the child changes her mind, and uncovers
the buried seeds, one by one, small and soiled.
The lost and forgotten shall make a child's garden.

Sampler

The lawn is blue beneath the apple blossoms,
forget-me-nots clouding the little hill,
reflecting the sky, as water will,
and all around, the idle grass.
No sheep graze here, no shepherd
asleep in his heavy cape,
against his ear, the compressed forget-me-nots.
How eternal the castle of the master appears,
the stone tower doubled in the moat.
But the water's concentration is broken
by the slightest wind, a trout rising,
a peasant washing a new lamb.

The hands that stitched forget-me-nots
across this sampler have long been still.
A composition too fine to be a first effort.
The quiet work, perhaps, of late pregnancy,
awaiting confinement, consciousness
striving to double itself,
pain equal to the miracle.
Beneath the last bloom, worked in one thread:
Rebecca C., 1884, "Remember Me."
I do wonder, lifting the ancient linen,
how it is the blossoms are still sound.

All I've ever learned I've slowly forgotten,
a syllable each hour, till my cells
are clear as ice cubes.
Yet early summer comes,
a clutch of eggs in every hopeful nest,
a season unsuited to tragedy.
And in the crepuscular hours the closed flowers open
or the open flowers close, like shops for the bees.

Day Lilies

If these yellow day lilies
made the sound suggested by their anatomy
we couldn't have them in the garden . . .
great gold horns
on stems that would support them,
like some stage mother, on a world tour.
But they're rooted here in the red clay,
noisy only by virtue of their color
and posture, that desperate leaning away
from the leaves, that sun hunger.

Perhaps they know they have only one day.
One cool morning, a wind off the lake,
and one noon under a sun
that returns the most ardent affection.
One evening watching the shadows
of the porch spindles lengthen without tangling . . .
and the day is done. A day
that might have been worse or better,
that was never ours alone
though it seemed so.

Spring Recital

The nuns urge their pupils to the stage, to the huge black piano, as to a great fat uncle whose pardon they must beg. How clumsy young children are in those hard shoes! What weak little fingers they have! They press the white keys down against enormous resistance. The piano, the tall bench where their legs swing freely, the steps, this room, the world—all proportioned for the fully grown. This occasion, especially, is not strictly for their benefit.

All afternoon the obvious continues to occur. A music book falls, a slip shows, paralysis sets in, the notes swim like tadpoles through suppressed tears. The audience smiles at the earnestness of the incompetent but charmingly diminutive musicians.

Or perhaps one child does well. Eyebrows rise. It is the daughter of that hopelessly dressed woman in the second row, the one with graying hair that cannot be subdued by ordinary means. The woman whose head bobs in time to the fluid Chopin issuing from the piano (whose heart the little girl has won). Her fingers are like new flight feathers fluttering over the keys. The audience is astonished; the applause not merely polite.

It's seldom difficult to tell whose child is on stage. "Detached amusement" and "bored tolerance" disappear instantly. The parental organism is alert, almost alarmed, as if the child were drifting on that flimsy life preserver over the deep end of the pool. The fingers which this morning combed her fine gold hair now tremble. Perhaps they are held against the lips to prevent some outcry. Perhaps the father chooses this moment to rise and take a snapshot.

In my own case, I feel the same lightheadedness my daughter feels, the same sense of the full-color nightmare, the same swoon. I see the steps where her feet must perform their limited but crucial role. I feel the damp palms she rubs on her skirt. I feel the stricture where her blouse is taut across the shoulders.

But she's one of the older ones now. She's a tree that no longer needs staking. Light comes in from the west windows, and brilliant specks appear on the edges of chairs, the vase on the piano, the barrette in her dark hair. I have heard this music many times; I know every note. Is it beautiful? I can't tell anymore. Yes, yes, it's beautiful.

The man in front of me whispers to his wife that his clubs are in the trunk. She frowns. But after intermission his chair is empty. It makes very little difference where he is. The children take their bows, one by one, and as the program closes, the nuns remind everyone that volunteers are still needed for the annual Feast of the Arts fete two desperately short weeks away.

The Wandering Sky

It's the wind that drives the sky to one side
and herds the stars along, and pulls
the thread out of the needle.
A lifetime frugally spent
but gone all the same, and the chair,
that has become your tame little horse
tethered beneath the wandering sky—
the grandchildren dash through the room
like comets leaving a brilliant trail.
They have left the door wide open
but the wind will close it.

Wherever we go the clouds have preceded us.
Clouds of the vast transformation.
Thin clouds that thinly cross the bald dome.
Clouds like fishbones, like ribs
protecting the lung of the atmosphere.
Sometimes there are long words in the sky,
a sentence finished beyond the horizon.

Part Two

Truffles

Truffles lie on the plate
like the silk purse from a sow's ear.
They were growing between the oak's toes.
I myself have never tasted truffles.

A northern rain falls on my garden
and it suits my mood.
The awning sags, and the Great
fawn-colored Dane rests his head on his paws,
sad dog, feeble as a king
after generations of inbreeding
or too many truffles.

And yet truffles: breakfast on a terrace
beside the sea, cool shade, warm sun,
bougainvillea espaliered on the white stucco
like the beautiful woman who shows herself
slightly capable of compromise . . .
yes, she will share your truffles.

And the pig, for whom truffles are the Holy Grail,
forever desired and forever denied,
what of the pig?
After a sleepless night he rubs his small red eyes
and watches the moon go down.
In the absence of truffles
he would be satisfied with the moon.

Broom

A blossom on its long stem
the broom is a hag of a tulip.
It is a woman who ties back
her hair with wire,
who wears burlap,
who eats clay.

For its fidelity
the broom has been granted
the ability to carry the witch
to the clouds. Who was the first
to slip it between her legs
and vanish?

Skim Milk

The weary cow barely made the barn
and the farmer cleaned her withered udder
with little hope; but lo, a few drops,
a cupful, and at last a carton
of this Spartan beverage . . .
tempting, as self-flagellation is tempting.

Skim milk, reconstituted perhaps
from the dried granules, the little milk seeds
we distribute to developing nations
when what they need is pure butterfat
that lines the soul like a nest,
that recalls the sun, summer meadows . . .
buttercups . . . butterflies. . . .

Forget summer. The doctor hands you a stern menu
and the brilliant little lamps of pleasure
burn out one by one, irreplaceable.
Years stretch ahead, lean and dim,
like so many glasses of skim milk,
and the sad old cow looks up sympathetically,
her mouth full of thistles.

Dice

I prefer to avoid the singular form,
a solitary cube on the unlucky palm
resting over an abbreviated life line,
evidence of a failed marriage,
an infacility with houseplants,
especially ferns. I like two dice
rattling in the hollow of clasped hands
like a pair of provocative seeds.
Two dice waltzing in the plaza dust
surrounded by excited men.

Each is like a tooth,
hard and white with small decays,
a wisdom tooth, unwise but impressively sized.
(American advice: In all things choose large.)

I own some dice made of bone,
surprisingly lightweight, porous,
formed in some foreign country I think,
where everything is put to use,
but the rules are opposite—
seven is evil; girl babies a great misfortune.

Hour follows hour as the dice tumble.
I have written it all down, looking for a pattern.
The dice chatter like twins, shy with strangers
but accustomed to stares.
Back in a private pocket, they laugh and laugh.

Aesop's Sea Gulls

The gulls are too early.
Help! Help! they cry over the frozen harbor.
By nature entrepreneurial, they're seeking
public funding till the smelt run.

A child holds aloft a french fry
and they're on him, a scrum of gulls
bickering like politicians.
Now bold, now obsequious,
they flatter him out of his last morsel.

When they soar between us and the sun
we envy them, their lack of conscience.
Their shadows rush across the sand to touch us,
then zigzag over the frozen lake, the ice scab.
Heavy with books, we find a dry seat
on a rock, like two judges.

They're still arguing, circling clockwise, counterclockwise,
accusations, rebuttals, protestations of innocence!
How white are their feathers in the spring sky;
fleece white, or powdered like wigs.
As we offer them nothing, they abandon us, asserting:
Those with wings have no need of morals.

Radish

In this cold clay thrives a hot little vegetable,
the radish, the sensualist. When you wash it,
letting water trickle over its swollen root,
you make it very happy.

When you're dull, pull half a dozen.
They're crowded anyway,
gaining weight on all this rain.
Eat them red and plain.

Or eat them sliced and white.
Bite them and they bite you back—
you like that; resistance sharpens the appetite.
Attribute this blush to the effect of radishes.

Marbles

Certain eyes are this clear
but not this fixed,
and you can't finger an eye
as you can this marble.

It's a seed for a marble garden
with translucent blossoms
and ungainly pods bulging
like the toe of your sock.

It's a moon in the mutable universe
strewn across the carpet.
We are awed by our own hugeness,
by our enormous thumbs.

We divide the planets,
please ourselves by watching them collide,
as if there were no right or wrong,
only amusement or boredom.

Radiator

Mittens are drying on the radiator,
boots nearby, one on its side.
Like some monstrous segmented insect
the radiator elongates under the window.

Or it is a beast with many shoulders
domesticated in the Ice Age.
How many years it takes
to move from room to room!

Some cage their radiators
but this is unnecessary
as they have little desire to escape.

Like turtles they are quite self-contained.
If they seem sad, it is only the same sadness
we all feel, unlovely, growing slowly cold.

Minnesota Insects

Under the dinner table
among a dozen bare legs
a single giddy mosquito.

A blue moth lands on a violet
to exchange its damaged wings
for petals.

In a third-floor window of a derelict mansion,
a hornets' nest, like a gray urn.
Who can maintain such a dwelling?

I rest my hand on the spaniel's back—
under the hair, the braille of engorged ticks.
How the dog smiles at my expression. . . .

A ladybug comes in on the laundry.
Looking up at me, it offers to be a button
for a small remuneration.

The first hard frost followed by clear sun;
impatiens and insects, done.
How quiet, without the children.

Missed Bus

He sprinted around the corner to see it depart,
the flatulent yellow bus,
its windows inhabited by smug, successful faces.
A few noticed him,
his coat unzipped and only one mitten,
standing in a cloud of his own breath.
Failure is complete only when it is witnessed.

A little snow, so light it seemed not to fall
but to drift down, sideways, and up too,
pausing inquiringly before his eyes.
Perhaps the snow would eventually
end up on the ground. Or perhaps
it would be called back at the last moment
by a mother who insists
on a kiss in the middle of chaos.

The bus moves through the blue morning
lit up like a traveling theatre,
a shadow puppet in every window.
It always seems they are all against you,
shouting to the driver
"Leave! Leave! He's almost here!"

Cutting My Son's Hair

At nine years old his struggle
is premeditated, elaborate, cunning.
He volunteers to do his homework.

He negotiates like those specially trained police:
"Just put down those scissors, Ma'am,
and no one will get hurt."

"You think I like doing this?" I ask,
and he turns to me sadly.
"You're looking tired," he says. "Can't it wait?"

Standing with his shirt off
he watches his hair fall past his eyes.
Mouse-colored winter hair, lusterless.

Over and over I must ask him
to stay perfectly still, as if he were in danger.
But when the scissors close, he does not cry out.

"I'm sorry, but I can't have you going
to school looking like a wild man—
this is Minnesota." And he says, "I hate school."

Practical Pig Attends a CPR Class

It's hard to pinch a snout properly.
Everyone took a turn, but I was best.
I took all the handouts
plus two sets for my brothers.
I've been reading a medical book,
all the things that can go wrong.
I've begun to feel my organs
in a remarkable way,
a pancreatic hum, tiny bladder shocks.
Just before I sleep
I count the heartbeats
I feel in my ear.
I have a mole on my left shoulder
that seems to be growing.
After we learned CPR
they tested my blood cholesterol.
Mine was average for pork.

Luck

Beauty, brains, talent, luck . . .
the undemocratic distribution,
the uneven dispersement,
as of seeds down the carrot row.
(You read about the tycoon
who grudgingly bought one raffle ticket
from the emaciated Cub Scout at the door
then sold the brand new pickup
without even slipping behind the wheel.)
The force of luck moves like a breeze
through clover, a wave that heaves the keel
off the sandbar, wildfire
turning away in sight of the house,
a kind of lethargy that makes you
too late for the doomed plane.
Lucky people don't need maps,
or owner's manuals, or Roto Rooter.
They're the beneficiaries
of the world's life insurance policy
which they've never even heard of.
The rest of us carry this
repulsive rabbit's foot, toss salt,
scour the corroded horseshoe with Coke,
rub the stomach of some fat plastic troll,
dangle crystals from our earlobes.
And yet luck, that capricious guest,
declines the cocktails and hurries off
before the first course is served.

Duluth, Minnesota

A moose has lost his way
amidst the human element downtown,
the old-timers waiting out January
at the bar, the realtors and bureaucrats
with their identical plumage
(so that you must consult your Roger Tory Peterson)
hopping up the steps of City Hall
eating Hansel's bread crumbs—
poor moose, a big male who left
his antlers somewhere in the woods.
He keeps checking his empty holster.

People suffer the winters
for this kind of comedy.
Spectators climb the snowbanks,
dogs bark, the moose lowers
his shaggy head, his grave eyes
reminiscent somehow of Abe Lincoln.
Firemen, police, reporters, DNR,
two cents worth from every quarter,
till the moose lopes down Fourth Street
toward St. Mary's Hospital Emergency Entrance
and slips into an alley.

Later, the same moose—it must be—
is spotted farther up the hillside.
It's a mixed neighborhood; a moose
isn't terribly out of place.
And when he walks calmly up behind
one old man shoveling his driveway,

the Duluthian turns without surprise:
"Two blocks east," he says,
"Then you'll hit a small creek that will take you
to Chester Park, and right into the woods."
He adds, *"Good luck, now."*

Pickpocket

An almost subliminal violation,
a wrong so deliberately casual,
a collision that became an embrace,
and he looked at you, in the eyes,
which is all you remember,
that and a slight pressure
as of too much blood in the chest
or the inception of a migraine.
Where is he when he looks at what he's taken
without mercy, without tenderness?
A hotel room, an apartment,
the bathroom in a bar, his car,
the end of the pier—
out there, surrounded by waves,
would he think even briefly of you?
Or is it all reflex, autonomic,
a function of the brain stem?
The gulls think he's feeding them
when he sidearms the evidence
into the insatiable sea.

Part Three

Blue Moon

For the sisters Jacobson

This August a complete restoration, a blue moon.
It hesitates when it sees all of us
gathered here, watching. What can I do,
it says, but simply rise. . . .

The day was so fair, so blonde,
and the great lake becalmed, inviting
a hardy swimmer and his dog.
Inside the body the heart throbbed
like an engine of Swedish manufacture,
strong enough for a second lifetime.

A single cloud made the sky seem bluer,
one cloud against such odds.
True, we seldom see a day so unblemished,
so childish, so soon over.
Let us meet on the rocky shore
to ask this rare, self-conscious moon
to intercede on our behalf.

The lake lifts and sinks
like a sleeping father's chest, so gently
that small craft venture forth.
The stars, too, sense no danger in the heavens.
Our small fire burns only the sticks we give it;
we have that much control.
The moon returns with no assurances
but spreads a little light on the footpath.

The Gelding

As I recall, the black horse just appeared,
undelivered, unrequested,
dusty and skinny, like a tramp
with his hat in his good hand.
He was used to pity. He could work with it.

His dull eyes were rimmed with red,
and his habits were all bad:
he bit, suddenly and cruelly,
with his ears back flat.
He kicked the yearling squarely
in the ribs, so thoroughly
did he despise innocence.
The sweet filly he tried to mount
there, in the pasture, knowing we watched.
And we added to his scars
as everyone who owned him did.

Only once I forced him to take the bit
and slipped onto his bony back.
He seemed to acquiesce, then
threw himself into the fence.

If an animal can't be used one way
it will be used another.
So they came for him,
four strong men, armed with cigarettes,
leather, rope, a blindfold,
in a truck barred like a jail.

The black horse fought as if
he smelled a place they'd been.
Or as if this had been a fine home.
Trussed in, he was at last becalmed.
Almost bored. The truck rumbled away,
its blue exhaust drifting into the cornfield.

Up in the Night

Each night the clouds roll through
like nocturnal migraines, a flickering
in the periphery of half-closed eyes,
rain unusually warm for late August,
the air at body temperature . . .
so we feel inside out, somehow,
like insects exposed during their costume change,
egg to grub, or grub to wet-winged moth,
struggling out of our damp sheets,
more exhausted than the genuine insomniac
with his mysterious fuel.

The rain is an ineffectual punishment,
a whipping with a long white scarf.
It strips the clematis of its purple petals
and drowns a lost bee
sheltered in the child's watering can.
But we are not sorry
and we will never mend our ways.
Rain falls on the fresh paint
and the yet to be painted,
falling through the hours
like a recitation of petty confessions
our lawyers must scurry to retract.
Let the consequence be sleep.
Let the end of the interview be sleep.
Let the last word be sleep.

September

The last wild raspberry
falls before my outstretched fingers.
Each weed sends aloft
a kindergarten of seeds.
Now ripen the fruits
it took all summer to form:
apples thumping on the orchard floor,
rose hips swelling among the mildewed leaves.

Guests load their station wagon and depart,
while the cat, gone since May,
peers in at the screen door.
We are unlikely compass points
employed by such navigators,
we who cannot budge
(because of the piano).

How I love these September days
and nights when the wind
rocks the empty birdhouses.
What is alive lives still,
exhaling as the first flakes fall—
no two identical, like lost earrings.

Prayer

Her last well day she went apple picking.
Bushels of muddy windfalls for sauce
rot in the kitchen, covered with newspapers.

In the hospital she leans on the IV tripod
trying to walk. Everything computerized.
Everything expressed as zero or one.
One means alive.

After surgery, an old body with a new scar.
She shows it off; it's sensational.
She's confident now, broken parts fixed. She boasts
"In my mother's day I'd have died from this."

Died in some quiet, darkened room
tended by daughters.
Boiled water, white cloth, willow bark, prayer,
muslin billowing at the window,
wind filling the room.

A window.
It's been a long time since she watched
the whole day pass without getting involved.
Today a thunderstorm at dusk,
people running to their cars
with newspapers over their heads.
Smoky asphalt, flaxen lawn
colors intensified by the rain
like rocks in a stream, each a gem.

One-Sided Pines

I stand a long time in the fog
but unlike these pines, I don't have to.
What is the opposite of a tree?
Perhaps wind, bodiless, endlessly mobile,
a tourist without a motel,
an element with a short attention span.
The pines sigh deeply when the wind comes.
Is it envy? Resignation?
Is it that almost parental disapproval,
sapience confronting naiveté, right
in the face of very, very wrong?

Some of these pines
have branches on one side only,
something I've always blamed on the wind.
They seem to be moving in the fog
the way huge things move, imperceptibly,
the way the sun is drifting
out of the center of the planets.

Perhaps it's impossible to reach that age and size
with all one's branches intact.
Little clear drops hang on the end of each needle
like something medicinal;
when the air stirs the tree responds
with its own local rain, a personal tragedy
repeated across the hillside.

The wind is not so much wrong as immature,
that recklessness that takes its toll on the elderly.
   "When it was over my hair had gone
   from brown to white."
And by the first light I see
the wreckage of many branches in the spring mud,
chickadees guarding their fallen nests,
squirrels whose world has been turned
upside down.

                One-sided pines.
I feel like a small, frail thing beside them,
a child again, pale against the rain-dark trunks,
the lofty limbs directing me south-southeast,
gesturing this way, that way, approximate instructions
for a cheerful, productive life.
The wind makes my eyes water
but the trees go on saying the same words,
   "If I'm not here when you get back. . . . "

Dragonfly

A dragonfly visits me as I take down the laundry.
He clings to a sleeve like a mighty cuff link,
gold and purple, with four sluggish wings
the shape of willow leaves, and will not fly.
No, he has found the last sun
that stains the garment and the day, and will not fly.

Night stands with its goods at the door,
impatient to inhabit summer's mansion,
like the unsentimental purchaser on closing day.
You lead him through the empty rooms a last time
and give him the key. Somewhere a window left open . . .
and the cold rushes in.

The moon seems always in the sky, night or day.
All life ends under such a fierce moon,
sharp-tipped as an Abyssinian sword.
What are your thoughts, dragonfly,
as my finger comes so near?
Do you feel the furnace of my red blood?
Can you trust me? I could put you in a jar
decorated with clematis, a pleasant room,
a windowsill, a button to push for the nurse.
But no, you seem to say no,
as you throw yourself into the grass.
I see worn places on your wings
just as every leaf in the woods
has its caterpillar hole.

After our talk, we let each other go.
In a few steps I enter the shadow of the house
which rises on me like a watermark.
All over the sky the nighthawks
are crossing through the visible spectrum.
And the day, like a last penny
pulled from deep in the pocket, is spent.

This Windy Day

I warm my hands on my coffee cup
and think of my father
lifting floundering sow bugs
out of the swimming pool.
If he had a tiny towel
I think he'd help dry them off.

When we lived nearby
he'd visit on his bicycle
a bag of oranges in his basket
and he'd hold one up—a miracle!
How could a tree do this?

Clouds warm their hands
on the rising sun, then move off.
Families of clouds don't necessarily
stay together.

This windy day
the children and I go walking
through streets deep with leaves.
We talk about Grampa, how we miss him.
But children feel things differently—
swift, sharp, a side-ache.
Then they're running again
shoelaces untied, leaving us behind.

Maple Wings

1.

The wind has shifted, carrying along
the odor of the Superwood plant—
trees as organ donors,
Grand Tetons of sawdust.
Down by the knotted railroad tracks,
industry's complex signature,
ore docks, grain elevators,
chain link fences holding back empty shoreline
where slender white fish
wash up among the pitted rocks.
Through the fall trees
we begin to see the eye of the lake
looking back at us.
The lake does not distinguish innocence from guilt.
It touches the whole shore
then shrinks back everywhere.

2.

Maple wings are falling
a thousand an hour.
They land in the birdbath,
in the geranium pot; they spin
into the open car window.
The children fill their pockets
and scurry up to the balcony
to fling the maple wings off.
Of this plenitude
nothing will come.
But the moment itself comes
like the strike of a single match
added to the sun.
All night cold pours down from the heavens
through the ozone hole.

3.

I was wrong.
Here is a maple seedling
among the frozen petunias.
Three leaves already, precocious.
Leaning over it, I see my white breath vanish.
A baby born as winter begins, a late lamb.
"In those days," Grandma said,
"You never got attached. You tried not."
The uncombed grass lies down,
the wind takes the leaves,
the lake swallows the sun.
But we are attached. We already are.

Rain

When the rain comes
you don't try to stop it.
You don't give it a final warning.
It comes, and the plants look up
and hold up their leaves.

It is the age of parents failing,
asleep in the afternoon, awake in the night.
The first light enters the east window
trying to make the nerves come alive
like leaves growing from a stump.

When the grandchildren visit
each must suffer an inspection, a silly joke
and the reverent touch of the old hands—
how hard it is to love and be loved!

Rain, come out of the milky sky
and wash the dust from the bird wings!
There is no reason for anything
yet we live.

Part Four

Toward Dusk

My hand on the gate
I look back into the garden.
My shadow lingers between the rows
and pulls the shadow of a weed.

The seedlings are thick stemmed,
well begun. Should I not return
they would still grow, these delphiniums,
blue eyed, my height and a little beyond.

It wasn't my fate after all
to do more than plant
at the proper phase of the moon,
and love what grows.

St. Hans' Night

*"Soon there began to be no night; the sun barely dipped
his face into the sea and then came up again, red,
refreshed, as if he had been down to drink. . . . "*
—Knut Hamsun

All day sunlight sank into the water
and held its breath.
White feet, too, startled the minnows
with their ignorant meanderings.
One knows the world, yet is
continually astonished.
And night, if night it can be called,
has held the afternoon
by its white, warm hand,
and now they are walking into the trees
while on the bright water boats drift.

The light has made us weak.
We lie in the sand beside overturned boats,
their wet keels shining,
and they seem to be breathing slowly,
resting like seals, resting as we rest
between one passion and another.
Around the bonfire people eat and drink and call to us.
The shadow of the woods stretches toward our bare legs.

Once we entered those woods, you and I,
while wind lifted the leaves
to see their white undersides.
Perhaps the bark was a little rough
where we leaned, and the warm grass
made us sleepy. Perhaps

our skin tasted slightly of salt
and the human smell was stronger
than the wild lupine.

After midnight it is morning
and still no moon.
Two loons surface suddenly in the calm water,
the way we wake up after not sleeping.

Special Ride

A whisper woke me. My father,
urging me to dress, to steal away with him,
leaving mother and the others,
the rest of the litter. Children came like that
in those days, one a year,
four or six or eight in all,
and parents were bewildered,
I have to believe, by what they'd done.
Our dog, Lady, shook off the puppies
sometimes, just to stand alone
by the back door. When we opened it for her,
she thanked us, but declined.

We snuck into the cold car
and drove into town, Sunday morning,
past the church ablaze with early Mass.
It was Lent, but Father said,
what was there left to give up?
We ate blueberry crepes at the hotel,
then walked past dark storefronts
to the only place open, the drugstore,
where Father bought pipe tobacco.
I chose licorice whips for all, and for Mother
a white plastic vase, with plastic violets.
They'd be dressed for church by now,
fasting for Communion.

The sun was high as we passed
fields of corn stubble, empty barns
and full ones. I was a girl
who inspected every landscape for horses.
If I was ever to own one,
it would be Father who'd say yes,
Father of indulgences, of "special rides"
for this week's royal child.
He gestured me close
and let me hold the steering wheel
as he tended the pedals.
There were two ways home,
one long, one longer.
And the way I go now.

Hollyhocks

1.

Did you think you were to have your pleasure
all at once? No, there is a season for happiness,
a kitchen window opened and reopened
until the hollyhocks are tall enough to see in,
to greet the invalid.

2.

There came a time when the philanderer
had to throw himself upon the mercy
of the one he had wronged.
How symmetrical fate can be!
She forgave him, but God was stern.
God claimed the half of his body
that had told half truths. After his stroke
he lifted the bad hand with the good
and struck the table, shook the table,
but could no longer articulate the curse.

Yet she forgave him,
wheeled him from bed to table
like a fleshy child in a stroller.
Like a naughty child
who was made an example of . . .
Why oh why had God made the girls so pretty?
They were bait in a celestial trap
disguised as a boudoir.
They were the yellow cream
that turns bitter coffee delicious.

3.

Year after year she raked off the leaf mulch
to see the fresh, eager growth
from roots everlasting. Hollyhocks,
robust, immaculate, confident,
full of a power they never requested.
It was the power of regularity,
the power of habit and duty,
of kindness when cruelty is warranted,
the power of unmerited happiness.
The power of the whole earth majestically turning
while we lie awake.
One after another the blossoms opened,
each a separate revelation,
a series of doors through which one passes
at the trial's conclusion,
after the guilty are found innocent.

Peonies

It is winter before we think clearly
of the peonies. Wind rearranges
a light snow over their roots,
filling the faint tracks of the neighbor's cat.
The wind has forgotten why it feels so unhappy.

I remember that mild June night
we sat out waiting for the moon,
and fireflies appeared like broken pieces of it
drifting over the peonies.
The flowers had a light of their own
and regarded the world as infants do,
full of great, unknown capacity.

The white peony was cooler than the air.
When I took it in my hand
and held it near your face
I saw your unguarded, nocturnal features,
simple and irrational.
I believed then in what cannot be touched.

The sun rose on peonies
throwing away their petals
as nuns conceal their hair and bodies.
They had served their short time
in the physical world.
Now it is the snow that falls
in great soft petals, spent blossoms
on the year's darkest day.

Smoked Fish

I thought myself unfamiliar with death.
Then I unfolded the butcher paper.
It was the whole trout, including
that swollen eye, a gilded thing,

alive yesterday. Its mouth
seemed pugnacious, open a little,
retracting the three wishes.
Severing negotiations altogether.

I looked past the ivy on the windowsill;
my breath steamed the cold glass.
Snow, and a wind that kept it moving.
Can death be the only thing that does not end?

I felt we should eat the fish, and we did,
careful of the bone needles, wasting nothing.
Finished, we washed away
the gold scales that clung to our fingers.

The Lights of the Valley

The lights of the valley have multiplied each year
like cells of the body slowly dying.
The doves fly up from a field
where they will not return.

When the sun descends, our darkness is beginning,
the darkness of the automobile, rushing into its own light.
What creature watches near the highway, transfixed,
about to step forward?

Mistletoe

You carried your youngest on your shoulders;
"Up so high!" And he held your hair in his fists
as he might grasp the horse's mane,
you, the mute beast of burden
searching for your car in the murky lot
two levels down from the surface of the earth.
Sing a little Christmas song and the child
joins in; pretend you are in the country,
walking along an irrigation ditch
beside the almost native trees,
the besieged Chinese elms, draped with mistletoe.

They must have seemed the perfect desert tree:
long rooted, small leafed, each offering
billions of weightless seeds to the wind,
seeds that drifted like sand against the door.
The lusty saplings leapt from the center
of the dense pomegranate, ferocious as young
capitalists, immigrants slaving for pennies
who, next year, would open their own stores.
In ten years elms lined the ditches,
intercepting water on its way to the cotton fields,
but dulled, now, by their own success.

And we live among the aging elms,
the brittle branches, a dark sap
staining the split trunk,
the parasitic mistletoe
plump as a succulent
in the crotches and armpits,
the tender, damp junctions
where the living being
first turns against itself.

You brought the children here to gather mistletoe
last year, or the year before.
"Don't eat the berries! They're poison!"
And the little one began to cry
and wanted to go home.
Birds eat the seeds and don't die.
Some things seem possible only for others.
And how many met beneath the mistletoe
for a strange, accidental kiss,
under the influence of mysticism, of memory,
of proximity to a poison,
and your shoulders brush as you part,
one into, one out of, the darkened room.

Amaryllis

A flower needs to be this size
to conceal the winter window,
and this color, the red
of a Fiat with the top down,
to impress us, dull as we've grown.

Months ago the gigantic onion of a bulb
half above the soil
stuck out its green tongue
and slowly, day by day,
the flower itself entered our world,

closed, like hands that captured a moth,
then open, as eyes open,
and the amaryllis, seeing us,
was somehow undiscouraged.
It stands before us now

as we eat our soup;
you pour a little of your drinking water
into its saucer, and a few crumbs
of fragrant earth fall
onto the tabletop.

Narcissus

Because we forced them
they capitulated and cut short
their dormancy, but they were as irritable
as anyone with insufficient sleep.

What they had to do they did quickly,
tearing apart their brown paper
as a child opens a gift,
sending up shoots so pale—like Greeks
assimilated to England, or like the English
stepping out of their Athens hotel
groping for their sunglasses.

But soon this was their kitchen.
They felt our eyes upon them,
our hourly solicitations; they began to linger
over their own flower buds,
swollen like breasts in a wedding dress.
In the mirror of the toaster
they watched themselves disrobe.

Beautiful, as expected.
But doused with a vile perfume
a healthy rain might have diluted.
We couldn't bear them
but couldn't throw them out. Not yet.
How slowly they aged, to spite us,
their petals white as camisoles,
their long leaves drooping
the way unpinned hair falls over an eye.

Christmas Tree

Five days after Christmas
we are weary of the tree.
Stale joy, a half-grown puppy.
No one waters it
or admires the lights;
the sharp spruce needles
drop onto the tree skirt,
through the holy chamber
the presents occupied, empty now,
things eaten and broken and read,
Christmas past. The ornaments,
gaudy and plain, are folded and stacked,
and the tree stands as it once did,
but dead. It's lovely anyway by itself,
like an empty house. Walking through
you notice wall shadows, door handles,
the hall floor like a river of oak,
and the windows, what is free to go out
and what is admitted at each pane of glass.
You notice your noisy shoes
and your enthusiastic, unnatural voice.
We own too much.

I am cleaning the old man's house.
Nothing of value. In the attic
boxes of Christmas decorations
the heirs do not wish to examine:
"Give it all to the poor."
Umbrellas lean in the corners,
the closets an impenetrable mass
of worthless retainees, the squalid pantry,
the predictably unclean bath—
but in the basement, jars of screws

arranged like a surgeon's tray
and a magnificent shortwave,
his audio window. Toward the end
the eyes always do fail.

We admire the tree anew, for one moment,
before dragging it into the snow.
Bitter cold is the forecast, dangerous wind chills,
one hundred percent chance of snow.
The tree will not suffer.
Wind will build a drift
over its northern branches, a pale, cold wall
rising, with little windows on the east.
Some creature may fly through these windows
which are always left open.
And here in the corner where the tree stood,
a chair, a lamp, a wastebasket.

January

Close the book. Close the blinds.
Close the door tight till the handle clicks.
Inside a walnut a white worm
gnaws whatever touches it.
The rooms are warm for the sick one,
in every corner the smell of fever.
We are nearly out of batteries.
Between us we have twenty pale fingers
to count each hour of the dark.

It is said the sun rises,
yes, like air trapped under the ice.
We can see it through the low clouds,
but it doesn't matter.
The winter is rich and we are poor—
yet the cold comes in
to finger the thin curtains.

2.

When I close my eyes
I see them clearly, the bathers
wading near the dock in the weedy water.
Behind them the summer hillside,
the pedigreed birches, popple
thriving like mongrels. I see them
clearly, the youngest up to her waist,
the mother standing at the water's edge
shading her eyes. I hear her thin call.
The older siblings, the boy and girl
who look so much alike at this age,
have undertaken a quest for minnows.
And what would you do with them?

Let them go. Capture them and let them go.
Hold them in the palm, have them,
and see that they feel as you would,
held under. They are like tiny
individual muscles. Their lips are transparent.
The flared gills dry like petals.
Drop them quickly so you can breathe again.

No one wants to sleep.
Raindrops splash on the lake
like handfuls of minnows.
The children feel feverish with sunburn,
sand in the crease behind their knees.
For hours the warm twilight
lingers in the woods, while
we sit on the porch in our white pajamas
like a cluster of mushrooms.
Someone speaks aloud the word *winter*
but no one believes in such a thing.
The darkness is so shy
it has stolen away before we wake.

Bonfire

After a simple meal, we wash with snow
and throw the bones on the bonfire.
Someone drags forward the remains
of the Christmas tree . . . rags, a suitcase,
a marriage certificate . . . then you rush close
and offer something from your pocket.
The great animal in the fire
stands on its hind legs
and rakes the air as it falls backwards.

The orange light is like
a scrap of cellophane over the scene,
sealing the exotic diorama:
the vast flames on this bitter January night,
and our hulking, primitive shapes
shifting, thrusting forth a long stick,
falling back as the bundle of manuscripts
at last has some effect.

Our faces, bearded and smooth,
darken as the fire dies, and the cold
clamp tightens on the little clearing.
Despite the new year, the heavens
use the same worn calendar.
But tonight, strange unreasonable hopes
stir in us like seeds planted
far in advance of the season.
What we have done so far isn't much,
but there is still time. . . .

Ski Tracks

1.

He left the trail here
heading for home as the crow flies—
ski tracks, one melody, one harmony,
and his meandering husky.
Straight through the brown ferns
past the sumac's red seed heads—
a little art nouveau
in the otherwise minimalist landscape.

Is this silence or exhaustion?
His skis lean against the cabin as snowflakes
drift through the porch light like moths.
This man is thin as a ski.
He boils fish and potatoes
that rise up as he stirs them
as if it is they who will be fed.

The stars look down hungrily
from their overpopulated sky
and sparks fly up from the chimney
equally unsatisfied.

2.

He built this cabin when his father died.
With the insurance money.
His wife left him when he quit his job.
"Don't keep in touch."
The gray in his beard
grew to resemble animal markings.

He thought of the woods as perfectly indifferent
then realized they were slightly irritated:
he was worse than a moose but
better than army worms.

Once he snowshoed out to the bar
and spent the night in an upstairs room.
He kept waking up. A car.
A barking dog. Even the phone lines
made a kind of whine. And that smell
of beer on the short napped carpet.
And the floor that gave a little with each step.

Sometime in the night the weather changed.
Heavy clouds, but warmer. Rotting snow.
Yes, it was like something once alive
once swirling like a skirt.
Now his snowshoes sank into the snow's corpse.
He tried to think of it as the opposite of death,
the water released like the genie out of the bottle.
He felt the clouds sinking.
It was warm enough to rain.

About the Author

Connie Wanek was born in Madison, Wisconsin, on June 1, 1952, and was raised in Las Cruces, New Mexico. She graduated from New Mexico State University in 1975. In 1990 she and her husband and two children moved to Duluth, Minnesota, where they work renovating old houses.

When she was at NMSU, Wanek served as poetry editor of *Puerto del Sol.* In 1990 and 1994 she was a winner of the Lake Superior Writer's Competition. She has been interviewed on radio for station KUMD's series of Northland Writers and on public television. The Arrowhead Regional Arts Council awarded her an Artist's Fellowship for 1997–98.

New Rivers Press's
Minnesota Voices Project Titles

Begun in 1981, the Minnesota Voices Project is a competition for the Upper Midwest's new and emerging writers. The series produces six books per year (poetry, fiction, essays, memoir) by residents of Minnesota, Wisconsin, the Dakotas, and Iowa who have not previously published a book with a commercial press.

1. *Household Wounds,* Deborah Keenan (poems)

2. *The Reconstruction of Light,* John Minczeski (poems)

3. *The Heron Dancer,* John Solensten (short stories)

4. *The Normal Heart,* Madelon Sprengnether Gohlke (poems)

5. *I Live in the Watchmakers' Town,* Ruth Roston (poems)

6. *Changing the Past,* Laurie Taylor (poems)

7. *When I Was a Father,* Alvaro Cardona-Hine (poetic memoir)

8. *Night Sale,* Richard Broderick (short stories)

9. *Casualties,* Katherine Carlson (short stories)

10. *Different Arrangements,* Sharon Chmielarz (poems)

11. *We'll Come When It Rains,* Yvette Nelson (poems)

12. *Rivers, Stories, Houses, Dreams,* Madelon Sprengnether (essays)

13. *Blenheim Palace,* Wendy Parrish (poems)

14. *Suspicious Origins,* Perry Glasser (short stories)

15. *Powers,* Marisha Chamberlain (poems)

16. *Morning Windows,* Michael Moos (poems)

17. *The Weird Kid,* Mark Vinz (prose poems)

18. *The Golf Ball Diver,* Neal Bowers (poems)

19. *Stars Above, Stars Below,* Margaret Hasse (poems)

20. *Matty's Heart,* C. J. Hribal (short stories)

21. *The Descent of Heaven Over the Lake,* Sheryl Noethe (poems)

22. *What I Cannot Say / I Will Say,* Monica Ochtrup (poems)

23. *Locomotion,* Elizabeth Evans (short stories)

24. *Twelve Below Zero,* Anthony Bukoski (short stories)

25. *Tap Dancing for Big Mom,* Roseann Lloyd (poems)

26. *Flash Paper,* Theresa Pappas (poems)

27. *All Manner of Monks,* Benet Tvedten (prose)

28. *The Wind,* Patricia Barone (novella)

29. *Holidays,* Lisa Ruffolo (short stories)

30. *Once, A Lotus Garden,* Jessica Saiki (short stories)

31. *Dying Old and Dying Young,* Susan Williams (poems)

32. *Storm Lines,* Warren Woessner (poems)

33. *The High Price of Everything,* Kathleen Coskran (short stories)

34. *Last Summer,* Davida Kilgore (short stories)

35. *Burning the Prairie,* John Reinhard (poems)

36. *The Transparency of Skin,* Catherine Stearns (poems)

37. *Turning Out the Lights,* Sigrid Bergie (poems)

60. *Handmade Paper,* Patricia Barone (poems)

61. *This House Is Filled with Cracks,* Madelyn Camrud (poems)

62. *Falling in Love at the End of the World,* Rick Christman (short stories)

63. *Thin Ice and Other Risks,* Gary Eller (short stories)

64. *The Peace Terrorist,* Carol Masters (short stories)

65. *Aerial Studies,* Sandra Adelmund Witt (poems)

66. *Mal D'Afrique,* Jarda Cervenka (short stories)

67. *Coming Up for Light and Air,* Barbara Crow (poems)

68. *What They Always Were,* Norita Dittberner-Jax (poems)

69. *Revealing the Unknown to a Pair of Lovers,* Ann Lundberg Grunke (stories)

70. *Everything's a Verb,* Debra Marquart (poems)

71. *Secrets Men Keep,* Ron Rindo (short stories)

72. *Heathens,* David Haynes (novella)

73. *To Collect the Flesh,* Greg Hewett (poems)

74. *Divining the Landscape,* Diane Jarvenpa (poems)

75. *The Dance Hall at Spring Hill,* Duke Klassen (short stories)

76. *Remembering China: 1935-1945,* Bea Exner Liu (memoir)

77. *On the Road to Patsy Cline,* John Reinhard (poems)

78. *Sustenance,* Aaron Anstett (poems)

79. *Fishing for Myth,* Heid E. Erdrich (poems)

80. *Self Storage,* Mary Helen Stefaniak (short stories)

Also Available from New Rivers Press

The Party Train: A Collection of North American Prose Poetry
Robert Alexander, Mark Vinz, and C. W. Truesdale, editors
ISBN: 0-89823-165-5

Tanzania on Tuesday: Writing by American Women Abroad
Kathleen Coskran and C. W. Truesdale, editors
ISBN: 0-89823-179-5

*American Fiction, Volume Eight: The Best Unpublished Short
    Stories by Emerging Writers*
Alan Davis and Michael White, editors, Charles Baxter, judge
ISBN: 0-89823-172-8

*New Rivers Press's books are sold to the trade by Consortium
Book Sales & Distribution, 1045 Westgate Drive, St. Paul, MN
55114-1065, 612-221-9035, 800-283-3572.*